LIFE

Wallace

Heinemann
LIBRARY

www.heinemann.co.uk
Visit our website to find out more information about Heinemann Library books.

To order:

 Phone 44 (0) 1865 888066

 Send a fax to 44 (0) 1865 314091

 Visit the Heinemann Bookshop at www.heinemann.co.uk to browse our catalogue and order online.

First published in Great Britain by Heinemann Library,
Halley Court, Jordan Hill, Oxford OX2 8EJ
a division of Reed Educational and Professional Publishing Ltd.
Heinemann is a registered trademark of Reed Educational & Professional Publishing Ltd.

OXFORD MELBOURNE AUCKLAND
JOHANNESBURG BLANTYRE GABORONE
IBADAN PORTSMOUTH (NH) USA CHICAGO

Designed by Celia Floyd
Originated by Dot Gradations
Printed by Wing King Tong, in Hong Kong

ISBN 0 431 10887 0 (hardback)
04 03 02 01
10 9 8 7 6 5 4 3 2

ISBN 0 431 10894 3 (paperback)
04 03 02 01
10 9 8 7 6 5 4 3 2 1

British Library Cataloguing in Publication Data

Wallace, Holly
  Food chains and webs. – (Life processes)
  1. Food chains (Ecology) – Juvenile literature
  I. Title
  577.1'6

Acknowledgements

The Publishers would like to thank the following for permission to reproduce photographs:

Bruce Coleman Collection: Jeff Foott pg.10, Andrew Purcell pg.19, Sir Jeremy Grayson pg.26; *FLPA*: E & D Hosking; *NHPA*: Ralph & Daphne Keller pg.4, Rod Planck pg.5, Nigel J Dennis pg.8, Michael Leach pg.9, Jany Sauvanet pg.11, Kevin Schafer pg.12, T Kitchin & V Hurst pg.13, Martin Harvey pg.13, Mark Bowler pg.17, Bill Wood pg.21, Laurie Campbell pg.22, B Jones & M Shimlock pg.23, B & C Alexander pg.24, Hellio & Van Ingen pg.28, R Sorensen & J Olsen pg.29; *Oxford Scientific Films*: Daniel J Cox pg.15, Michael Fogden pg.16.

Cover photograph reproduced with permission of Still Pictures.

Every effort has been made to contact copyright holders of any material reproduced in this book. Any omissions will be rectified in subsequent printings if notice is given to the Publisher.

Any words appearing in the text in bold, **like this**, are explained in the glossary.

Contents

Introduction

The six books in this series explore the features and life processes that keep plants and animals alive. *Food Chains and Webs* looks at the way in which the plants and animals in a particular place are linked together by what they eat. Because green plants can make their own food, they start off every food chain and web. All animals, including human beings, ultimately rely on plants for their food. The search for food takes up much of their lives.

Food and feeding

All living things must eat to stay alive. Food provides them with the energy they need to make new cells, grow and stay healthy. Green plants are able to make their own food by **photosynthesis** (see opposite). Animals cannot make their own food. They have to move about to hunt or **forage** for food. Some eat plants. Others eat animals that have fed on plants. In this way, they all depend on the food stored in plants to provide them with energy for their own life processes.

These sheep grazing on grass in Australia are 'primary consumers'.

Ecosystems and food chains

An **ecosystem** is made up of a **habitat** and the **community** of plants and animals that live in it. The plants and animals in an ecosystem react with each other and with their surroundings. They are linked to each other by their feeding habits. The energy produced by plants is passed on through the community in a food chain. Each link in the chain is food for the next in line.

Some food chains are quite straightforward. For example, in the Arctic, sea plants are eaten by fish that are eaten by seals that are eaten by polar bears. Within an ecosystem, many different chains link together to form a complex web.

Plant producers

Because green plants can make their own food, they start off every food chain. They are eaten by animals which may, in turn, be eaten by other animals. Plants are called **producers** because they use the Sun's energy to produce food. Animals that feed directly on plants are called primary **consumers** (the fish in our example). Animals that eat primary consumers are called secondary consumers (the seals). They may themselves be eaten by tertiary consumers (the polar bears).

Photosynthesis

Plants make food in their leaves, which contain a special green **pigment**, or colouring, called **chlorophyll**. The chlorophyll uses energy absorbed from sunlight to convert **carbon dioxide** from the air, and water from the ground, into a simple sugary food called **glucose**. This process is called photosynthesis. Oxygen is given off as a waste product. The food can be stored inside the plant's leaves, stems, fruit, seeds and roots until it is needed.

Sunlight

Carbon dioxide from air

Chlorophyll

Water from ground

Photosynthesis makes glucose from sunlight, water and carbon dioxide.

Did you know?

Many plants have special features to protect themselves from being eaten. Cacti, for example, grow in the scorching deserts. Their stems are covered in prickly spines instead of leaves. Large leaves lose water quickly, but spines help keep water loss to a minimum and keep hungry animals away.

The giant saguaro cactus of the USA stores water in its huge stem.

How food chains work

The living things in a **community** are linked together by what they eat. For example, plants are eaten by snails, which in turn may be eaten by birds. In this way, the energy produced by green plants is passed along the food chain. Some food chains have more links. For example, a bird may be eaten by a bigger bird or a fox. Animals that eat other animals are called **predators**. The animals that are eaten are called **prey**. Most **ecosystems** have a mixture of plants, predators and prey.

Food webs

Because animals often eat a mixture of things, they may appear in a number of different food chains. Within an ecosystem, these different food chains are linked together to form a food web. Our example food chain (plant → snail → bird → fox) is part of a larger, woodland food web. In this food web, the **producers** are the plants and trees. Animals such as snails and rabbits feed directly on plants and so are primary **consumers**. Birds that eat plants or seeds are also primary consumers. However, if the birds eat snails or rabbits, they are secondary consumers. The fox may be a secondary consumer if it eats a seed-eating bird or a tertiary consumer if it eats a snail-eating bird.

A woodland food web.

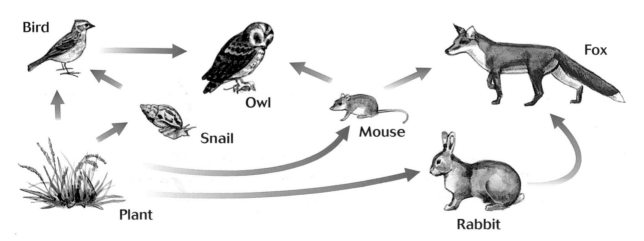

Bird

Owl

Fox

Snail

Mouse

Plant

Rabbit

Pyramid of numbers

The numbers of living things at each stage of a food chain can be shown using a diagram called a **pyramid of numbers**. In most ecosystems, there must be more plants than prey, and more prey than predators. For example, in the food chain above (plant → snail → bird), there must be more plants than snails and more snails than birds. Otherwise, neither the snails nor the birds would have enough to eat. You can show this information like this:

A simple pyramid of numbers.

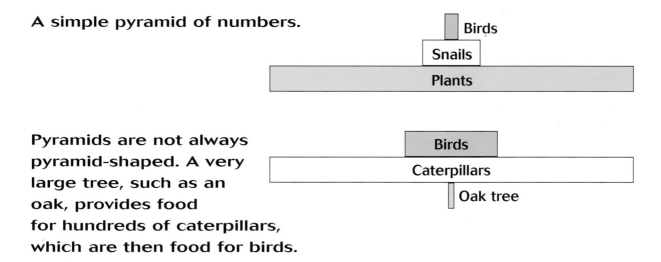

Pyramids are not always pyramid-shaped. A very large tree, such as an oak, provides food for hundreds of caterpillars, which are then food for birds.

Pyramid of biomass

The mass of living things at each stage of a food chain can be shown using a diagram called a **pyramid of biomass**. Biomass means the total mass of each type of living thing in the food chain. The pyramid of biomass for the oak tree food chain would look like this:

The pyramid shows how huge and heavy the single oak tree is, compared to all the caterpillars and all the

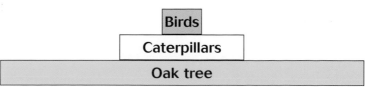

birds together. Its biomass is much greater than that of the caterpillars that feed on it. Likewise, the biomass of the caterpillars is much greater than that of the birds.

Herbivores

Herbivores are primary **consumers**. They are animals that live entirely on plants. They range from tiny insects that suck plant juices to huge elephants that uproot whole trees. Because their plant food is often not very nutritious, they have to spend a large part of their lives eating in order to get enough energy. They do not have to hunt for food because plants do not move about. But they often face fierce competition for food supplies from other herbivores.

Giraffes browsing on a knobthorn tree.

Grassland grazers

Grasslands around the world provide food for many different herbivores. They are able to live together because each animal eats a different part of a plant. On the African grasslands, animals such as giraffes and elephants eat the leaves from trees and bushes. They are called **browsers**. A giraffe's long neck helps it to browse on leaves high up in the trees. Other animals, such as zebras and antelopes, eat grass. They are called **grazers**.

Did you know?

African elephants have enormous appetites. These huge herbivores feed for about eighteen hours a day. Their skulls, teeth and jaws are specialized for crushing and chewing tough plant material. An adult elephant may eat more than 225 kilograms of grass, leaves, bark, flowers and fruit a day. Some male elephants may eat twice that much.

Eating seeds

Many birds are herbivores. Some eat fruit, nuts and seeds. Their beaks are specialized to suit their diets. Finches have short, strong, sharply pointed beaks for cracking open tough seed cases and reaching the food inside. Crossbills have unusual, crossed-over beaks for prising seeds out of pine cones. Parrots have very strong beaks for cracking nuts open. They use the hooked tips for pulling the soft pulp out of fruit.

A crossbill is adapted to eating seeds from pine cones.

Nectar drinkers

Every part of a plant – the roots, stem, leaves and flowers – provides food for a number of insects. Butterflies lay their eggs on plant leaves so that the caterpillars have plenty of food to eat when they hatch out of the eggs. Caterpillars can easily strip a plant bare. Adult butterflies suck up liquid nectar from inside a plant's flower with a long, hollow tube called a **proboscis**. It is coiled up when it is not being used.

Not being eaten

Many herbivores are eaten by birds and other animals who are secondary consumers in the food chain. Many herbivores have developed features to avoid being eaten. Some simply fly away. Others, such as stick insects, are perfectly **camouflaged** to look like the leaves or twigs they feed on. Some moths and caterpillars have eye-like markings to scare off hungry birds.

9

Carnivores

Meat-eating animals are called **carnivores**. They are the next link in the food chain. Carnivores are **predators** – animals that hunt other animals (their **prey**) to eat. They have special features for hunting and eating their prey. These may include sharp, pointed teeth and claws for gripping and tearing prey. Finding food can take a great deal of time and energy. Small carnivores, such as shrews, use up energy very quickly. They must eat their own weight in food each day, otherwise they will starve to death. Large carnivores, such as lions, need to eat much less in comparison.

Hunting in packs

Wolves are typical carnivores. They have large, dagger-like front teeth, called canines, for gripping prey. Between the canines are small, pointed incisor teeth for cutting through flesh. At the back of the wolf's mouth are its molar, or carnassial, teeth. These have sharp, scissor-like edges for slicing through tough hide, muscles and bone.

Wolves feed mostly on large mammals such as deer and moose. They hunt in well-organized packs, following a set plan of attack.

Anteaters

The giant anteater has a long, pointed snout and a long, sticky tongue for catching its prey of ants and termites. It tears open an ants' nest with its sharp, strong claws, then flicks its tongue in and out, lapping up hundreds of ants at a time. It needs to eat about 30,000 ants a day to get all the energy it needs.

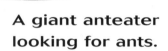

A giant anteater looking for ants.

Insect carnivores

Mammals are not the only carnivores. Many insects and fish are meat-eaters too. Robber flies are fierce predators. They perch on twigs, then pounce on other insects as they fly past. Then they suck out the insects' juices. Robber flies have hairy faces to protect their eyes from their prey, which may include stinging insects.

Scavenging for scraps

Some carnivores are **scavengers**. They eat prey that has died naturally or has been killed by another carnivore. Griffon vultures in Africa eat the remains of a lion's or cheetah's kill. They hover overhead until the lions have eaten their fill, then flock around the carcass. They can strip an antelope to the bone in just 20 minutes.

Did you know?

Some plants are also carnivores. The Venus fly-trap can make its own food by **photosynthesis**, but it eats meat to provide it with extra nourishment. This unusual plant has hinged leaves that lie open, waiting for an insect to land. Then they snap shut and dissolve the insect's body, using special digestive juices.

Omnivores

Omnivores are animals that can feed on both plants and meat. They include bears, rats, pigs, chimpanzees and human beings. Because omnivores feed on a wide variety of foods, they usually have no problem finding enough to eat. If one type of food becomes scarce they can usually find something else to eat. It also means that their teeth and other feeding features need to be less specialized than those of **herbivores** or **carnivores**.

A varied diet

Bears are mostly omnivorous, taking advantage of whatever food they can find. Depending upon where they live, their diet includes fruit, leaves, nuts, honey, small mammals and fish. Spectacled bears from South America eat a particularly wide range of food. Their diet includes more than 80 different types of food, which include for example deer, birds, rabbits, fruit, flowers, cacti, orchids and moss.

A spectacled bear feeding on leaves.

Did you know?

Cockroaches are **scavengers**. They usually feed on dead or decaying plants. But in many parts of the world cockroaches have become pests, eating anything from scraps of food in kitchens to household rubbish. Moving between the two, they can easily spread disease.

Chimpanzee hunters

Chimpanzees eat a mixed diet, including leaves, buds, seeds, eggs and termites. But they also catch larger **prey**. Some chimpanzees are fierce hunters. They form well-organized groups to hunt for colobus monkeys or wild pigs. Any meat they catch is shared out among the whole group.

A chimpanzee digging for termites with a stick.

City living

Omnivores are extremely adaptable in their feeding habits. Red foxes are now common in many European towns and cities where they make their dens in parks and gardens. They eat whatever they can find. They hunt rabbits, birds and small rodents, and **forage** for fruit. They also raid dustbins for leftovers.

In North America, raccoons raid dustbins for people's leftovers.

Fussy eaters

The giant panda's diet is highly specialized. As much as 95 per cent of its food is made up of bamboo stems, branches and leaves. Many different species of bamboo grow in the panda's forest home, but each panda eats only a few of these species. To obtain enough energy to survive, the panda must spend up to fifteen hours a day feeding. This is because it can only digest about a fifth of all the bamboo it eats. But the panda is not a total herbivore – very occasionally it eats fish and rodents.

13

Woodland food chains

Woodlands and forests cover almost a third of the Earth's land surface. With plenty of trees and plants to provide food, they are the start of a great many food chains. **Temperate** forests grow between the tropics and polar regions. They have warm summers and cold winters, and contain mostly **deciduous** trees, such as oaks, maples and sycamores. **Boreal** forests grow further north. These are huge forests of **coniferous** trees, such as pine, spruce and fir.

Forest food web

The Eastern Mixed Forest is a great woodland region running down the eastern USA. Here, the boreal, coniferous forest of the north meets the temperate, deciduous forest. The forest contains more than 150 species of trees, including maples, beeches and pines. These are the **producers**. A wide range of animals relies on them for food.

An example of a North American mixed forest food web.

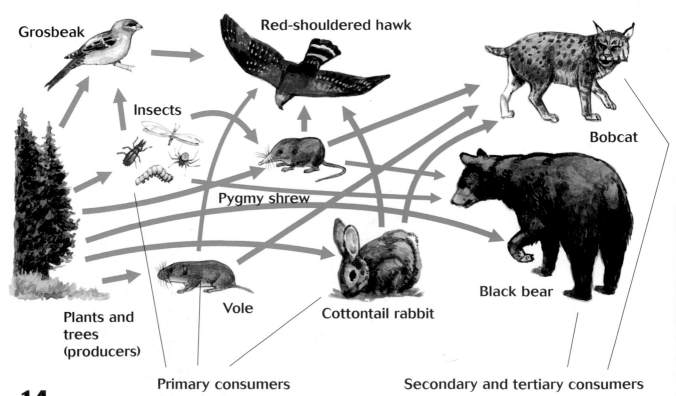

Grosbeak

Red-shouldered hawk

Insects

Bobcat

Pygmy shrew

Black bear

Vole

Cottontail rabbit

Plants and trees (producers)

Primary consumers

Secondary and tertiary consumers

Life in an oak tree

In an oak wood, a single oak tree provides homes and food for thousands of woodland creatures. Moth caterpillars, weevils and chafer beetles feed on the leaves. In turn, they provide food for birds, such as warblers. Acorns are eaten by birds, voles and squirrels. Dead leaves on the ground provides food for woodlice, worms and small mammals. Owls shelter among the branches and hunt mice and voles.

Forests in winter

In autumn, the leaves of deciduous trees change colour to red, yellow or orange as their **chlorophyll** starts to break down, allowing other **pigments** to show through. Then the trees shed their leaves. This allows them to survive the cold winter when it is difficult to suck water from the frozen ground and make food. The lack of leaves means that food is scarce for woodland **consumers**. Some, such as dormice, survive by **hibernating**. Others, such as squirrels, live off stores of nuts and acorns.

Did you know?

Koalas live in the eucalyptus forests of south-eastern Australia. Eucalyptus trees are **evergreen**, providing food all year round. Koalas feed almost entirely on eucalyptus, consuming more than 1 kilogram of leaves each day.

A koala feeding on eucalyptus leaves — its favourite food.

Rainforest food chains

Although rainforests only cover about a tenth of the Earth's land surface, they are home to at least half of all the world's species of plants and animals. They have the highest **biomass** of any **ecosystem** and the greatest variety of living things. Rainforests grow in layers, depending on the height of the trees. Each layer has its own **community** of plants and animals, and its own food chains. From the ground up, the layers are the floor, the understorey, the canopy and the emergent layer.

Forest floor dwellers

The forest floor is dark, gloomy and covered in a thick blanket of fallen leaves. These rot, or **decompose**, quickly and transfer their goodness back into the soil (see page 28). The leaves provide food for huge numbers of insects, and other creatures such as millipedes. Millipedes burrow through the soil and leaf litter, grazing on half-decayed leaves. If they are threatened, they curl up into a tight ball until the danger has passed. Small mammals feed on the insects and are in turn **prey** for larger **predators**, such as jaguars.

Did you know?

The beautiful flower mantis is an insect, perfectly **camouflaged** as a rainforest flower. Even its wings look like petals. This helps it surprise its prey. It stands on a twig, ready to shoot out its front legs and catch passing insects such as butterflies. Other mantises disguise themselves as twigs or leaves to avoid being eaten.

A flower mantis is cleverly disguised.

Beware – poison

The poison-arrow frog lives in both the understorey and the forest canopy. It feeds mainly on insects. To avoid being eaten itself by birds or snakes, the frog has deadly poisonous skin. Just one drop can kill a bird immediately. The frog's bright colours warn predators that it is very nasty to eat. Forest people extract the poison and use it to tip their hunting arrows.

Monkey-eating eagles

The tallest rainforest trees form the emergent layer, up to 60 metres above the ground. Here, large birds of prey, such as the monkey-eating eagle, make their nests. These huge predators hunt for prey in the next layer down, the canopy, diving and twisting through the branches after a troop of monkeys. They take their prey back to their nest to feed themselves and their young.

A monkey-eating eagle.

Rainforest herbivores

Many rainforest animals live in the trees, where leaves and fruits make up a large part of their diets. An orang-utan feeds mainly on rainforest fruits, such as figs, mangoes, lychees and durian fruit. Different trees produce fruit at different times of the year. The orang-utans have the amazing ability to remember which trees are in fruit at particular times and where they are.

An orang-utan.

Freshwater food chains

Only about three per cent of all the water on Earth is freshwater. The rest is salty and makes up the seas and oceans. Freshwater is found in rivers, ponds, lakes and marshes all over the world. Each of these **habitats** has an **ecosystem** with its own distinctive food chains and webs. In a freshwater food chain, the **producers** are water plants. These are eaten by thousands of tiny **invertebrates**, including insects, insect **larvae**, snails and shrimps, which in turn provide a rich food supply for many other freshwater creatures.

Pond plants

All freshwater animals depend, directly or indirectly, on plants for their food. Pond plants grow in zones around the edge of the pond (marginal plants), on the water (floating plants), or under it (submerged plants). They range from huge water lilies to microscopic **algae**. The plants provide not only food for the **consumers**, but also shelter and egg-laying sites for them.

A pond food chain.

Kingfisher — Tertiary consumer

Perch — Secondary consumer

Shrimp — Primary consumer

Zooplankton and **Phytoplankton** — Producers

Sun

18

Going fishing

Fish are food for many freshwater birds. Many of these have specially adapted feet and beaks to help them catch their food. A heron has long legs for wading into the water. It stands very still until a fish swims by, then grabs it with its long, pointed beak. A kingfisher is built for diving. It plunges into the water and stabs a fish with its sharp beak.

A dragonfly larva eating a worm.

Dragonfly diet

Insects live in every part of a freshwater ecosystem and play a vital part in the food chain. Many provide food for birds and other creatures. Some are **predators** in their own right. Adult dragonflies are skilful hunters, catching insect **prey** in mid-air. Their larvae live under water. They are also fierce hunters, preying on water fleas, tadpoles and even small fish.

Did you know?

Piranha fish live in the Amazon River in South America. These small but ferocious hunters are famous for their razor-sharp teeth. Piranhas attack their prey in **shoals**, becoming more frenzied as they feed. Their normal prey is dead or injured fish. But they can strip an animal as large as a cow to its bones in just a few minutes. Not all piranhas are **carnivores**. Some eat fruit and leaves that fall into the water.

Ocean food chains

The oceans and seas form an enormous **ecosystem** that covers about two-thirds of the Earth. A huge variety of living things is found in the oceans, on the surface and at every depth. As on land, plants and animals in the ocean are linked together by what they eat. There are thousands of different ocean food chains, which link together to form a massive and complicated food web.

Ocean plants

As on land, every ocean food chain starts with green plants. The ocean's primary **producers** are microscopic single-celled plants called **phytoplankton**. They are **algae**, the simplest type of plants. They grow in the top 150 metres of the sea, where sunlight can reach them and they can make food by **photosynthesis**. Phytoplankton are grazed on by tiny **herbivores** called **zooplankton**, which, in turn, provide food for larger **consumers**. Without phytoplankton, nothing could live in the sea.

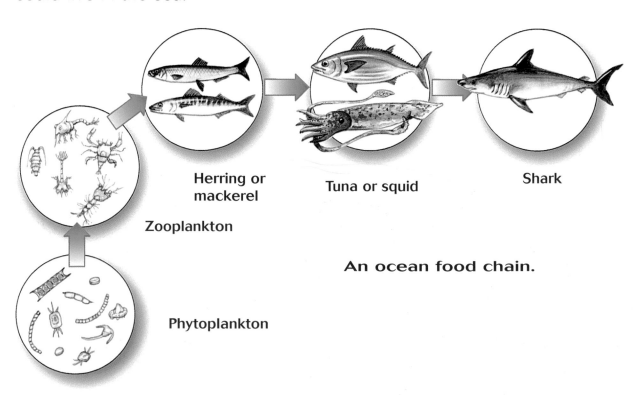

Herring or mackerel

Tuna or squid

Shark

Zooplankton

Phytoplankton

An ocean food chain.

Giant appetite

Some of the largest animals in the sea feed on some of the smallest. The gigantic blue whale feeds on tiny, shrimp-like creatures called krill, which are types of zooplankton. Krill live in vast **shoals**.

The blue whale sieves the krill out of the seawater using long, bristly **baleen plates** hanging down from the sides of its mouth. A blue whale may eat up to 4 tonnes of krill a day.

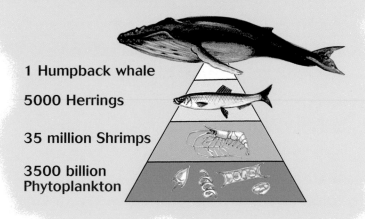

Ocean pyramid

A **pyramid of numbers** for the ocean might look like this one.

1 Humpback whale

5000 Herrings

35 million Shrimps

3500 billion Phytoplankton

Deep-sea features

In the depths of the ocean, it is dark and very cold. No plants can grow here because there is no sunlight for photosynthesis. As a result, food is scarce. Deep-sea animals must eat other animals or the remains of dead plants and animals that drift down from the surface. Many have special features to make the most of any food they find. Gulper eels, for example, have huge mouths and elastic stomachs for swallowing **prey** much bigger than themselves.

Did you know?

Sea cucumbers are sausage-like **echinoderms** that live on the seabed and feed on tiny scraps of food. They can shoot out streams of sticky guts, or **entrails**, that entangle hungry attackers. The entrails regrow within a few weeks.

A sea cucumber.

Seashores and reefs

Twice a day, the sea rises and floods the shore, then ebbs, or falls away, again. These changes in sea-level are called tides. Most seashore animals time their search for food to when the tide has gone out. Then there are rich pickings to be had.

Seaweeds

Like **phytoplankton**, seaweeds are a type of **algae**. They anchor themselves to rocks along the coast with a root-like holdfast. When the sea comes in, they float near the surface so that they can still absorb sunlight for **photosynthesis**. Small animals, such as sea-snails, graze on seaweeds.

Shore birds

When the tide is out, wading birds such as curlews and oystercatchers gather to feed on the shore. Oystercatchers use their long, strong beaks to prise open cockle and mussel shells. Curlews probe the sand and mud for shellfish and worms with their long, curved beaks.

Redshanks feeding on the seashore.

Coral reefs

Almost a third of all the world's fish species live around coral reefs. Reefs are home to thousands of creatures, from brilliantly coloured butterfly fish to enormous giant clams. Each creature has its own niche, or place, in the reef **ecosystem** and its own source of food.

Coral builders

Coral reefs are built by tiny polyps, related to jellyfish and sea-anemones. Like sea-anemones, coral polyps use stinging tentacles to stun or kill their **zooplankton prey**. The polyps build stony, cup-like cases to protect their soft bodies. When the polyps die, their cases are left behind. Corals can only grow in shallow, sunny water. This is because they grow in partnership with algae, which need sunlight in order to photosynthesize.

A coral reef provides a home for many animals.

Coral feeders

Many animals feed on the coral itself. Parrot fish get their name from their sharp, parrot-like beaks, which are formed by their front teeth. The fish scrapes away at the hard coral, then uses another set of back teeth to crush the coral up.

Did you know?
Parts of the Great Barrier Reef in Australia are being eaten away by the crown-of-thorns starfish. The starfish grips a piece of coral in its arms, then pushes its stomach out over it. It takes several hours to digest the coral. Then the starfish pulls its stomach in and moves on.

Food chains and you

What did you eat for your last meal? A pizza? A tuna fish sandwich? A bowl of cereal? Whatever you ate, it links you into a food chain or into a larger food web. Human beings are usually considered to be **omnivores**, eating both plants and animals. Our ancestors were hunter-gatherers. They hunted wild animals for meat, and gathered plants. Luckily, you no longer have to go out hunting. You can buy all the food you need in the supermarket!

Fish is an important source of proteins and oils.

A balanced diet

To obtain all the **nutrients** and energy you need, and to stay healthy, you require a balanced diet. This means including six vital types of food in your diet. These are:

- Carbohydrates – for energy. Found in bread, rice, cereals.
- **Proteins** – for growth and repair. Found in meat, fish, eggs, beans.
- Fats – for energy and warmth. Found in milk, cheese, butter, oils.
- Vitamins – for regulating chemical processes in your body. Found in fruit, vegetables, fish, milk.
- Minerals – for healthy cells. Found in fish, vegetables, fruit, milk.
- Fibre – for healthy digestion. Found in fruit, vegetables, wholemeal bread, bran.

Two food chains

If you are an omnivore and you eat a tuna fish sandwich, you form part of two food chains, one long and one short. In the first food chain, you are the fourth consumer in the chain. In the second, you are the primary consumer.

1 **Phytoplankton** → **zooplankton** → small fish → tuna → you
2 Wheat (the wheat is made into bread) → you

Vegetarians and vegans

Some people choose not to eat meat. Vegetarians eat vegetables, fruit, nuts, pulses such as lentils and beans, and grains such as wheat. They do not eat meat or fish. Some eat eggs and dairy products because this does not mean killing animals.

Vegans do not eat any animal products. This includes eggs, honey and anything that may contain animal fat. Vegans are always primary **consumers**. Vegetarians are usually primary consumers because they eat food that comes directly from plants. For example, the food chains for a cheese salad would look like this:

1 Grass → cow (the cow's milk is made into cheese) → you
2 Salad vegetables → you

Cycles in nature

In nature, nothing goes to waste. Everything is constantly being recycled and used again. When living things die, their bodies **decompose**. Other living things break them down into basic minerals and chemicals that plants can use to grow. In this way, the cycle begins again. **Recycling** is very important. If it did not happen, living things would run out of the things they need to grow.

Decomposers

Bacteria, **fungi** and some types of insects feed on the remains of animals and plants. They are called, decomposers and are found at every stage in every food chain. Decomposers break down dead plants and animals into **humus** and minerals in the soil. As they do so, they not only obtain the energy they need to live

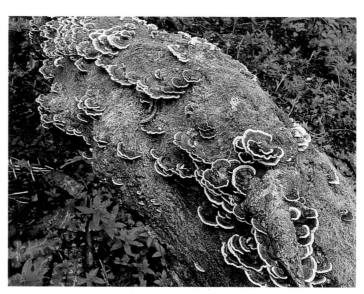

Fungi growing on a tree trunk.

but also enrich the soil so that plants can grow. Bacteria also release **carbon dioxide** into the air, which can be used by plants for **photosynthesis**. Decomposers are often left out of food webs and **pyramids of numbers** because it is so difficult to count or show them.

Feeding fungi

Fungi are neither plants nor animals. They belong to a third **kingdom**, or group, of living things. A fungus is made up of a mass of tiny threads called hyphae. The threads of hyphae branch over dead material, dissolve it, then soak it up. Fungi live on dead material, such as dead leaves or rotting tree trunks. They are called **saprophytes**.

Carbon cycle

Carbon is one of the basic elements that make up all living things. This is how the carbon cycle works:

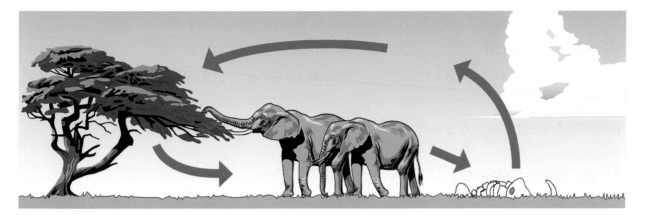

1 Carbon dioxide in the air
2 Plants use carbon dioxide to photosynthesize and make food
3 Animals eat plants and obtain carbon
4 Animals use carbon from plants for energy and growth
5 Animals produce waste and die
6 Decomposers feed on the dead matter and release carbon dioxide into the air as they respire

Nitrogen cycle

Living things also need **nitrogen** for growth. The basic nitrogen cycle is quite simple:

1 Green plants take in **nitrates** from the soil
2 Plants use nitrogen in these nitrates to build **proteins** for growth
3 When plants die, decomposers break the proteins down into **ammonium** compounds
4 Animals also eat the plants
5 Animal waste and dead animal carcasses are broken down into ammonium compounds
6 Bacteria in the soil can convert the ammonium back into nitrates

Upsetting the balance

The balance between **producers** and **consumers** in a food chain or web is a delicate one if there is going to be enough to eat. The balance can easily be upset or broken by natural and artificial means. If something happens to one of the links in the chain, it can be disastrous for all the others. For example, in a simple pond food chain, herons eat frogs that eat insects that eat plants. If the frogs were wiped out, the herons would not have enough to eat. With no frogs to eat them, the number of insects would increase. But there would need to be a greater number of plants to feed the insects.

When things go wrong

Poisons build up as they pass along a food chain. For example, DDT is a chemical sprayed on crops to kill insects. It was once widely used. But in the 1960s, scientists noticed an increase in eggshell thinning and death in some birds of **prey**, for example ospreys. They found that the ospreys contained large amounts of DDT. This is because the DDT was not **biodegradable**. It built up in the soil, then was washed into rivers and seas. There, it was taken up by **phytoplankton**, which were eaten by **zooplankton**, then fish, then ospreys. At each stage, the poison became more and more concentrated.

An osprey feeding its young.

Poisoned shellfish

The metal mercury is another poison that can enter the food chain with deadly consequences. In 1952, a chemical factory in Japan leaked mercury into the sea. More than 100 people died and thousands more were paralyzed by eating shellfish poisoned by the mercury.

Competition for food

The more food an animal can have, the better its chances of survival. But the more animals there are competing for a food source, the smaller the populations of those species will be. For example, if two types of animals are competing for grass, some will starve because less food is available for each of them.

Did you know?

Lemmings are small rodents from Norway. They feed on grasses, mosses and shrubs. They breed very quickly, putting great pressure on their food supplies. Every four years, there is a population explosion. The lemmings leave their homes in their thousands to search for more food. In their mad rush, many fall over cliffs or drown in the sea. This restores the numbers to a manageable size and life for the lemmings returns to normal – for a while, at least!

A Norwegian lemming.

Conclusion

All living things need regular supplies of food to fuel their bodies, help them to grow and keep them in good working order. In a particular **ecosystem**, food passes from plant to animal, and from animal to animal, along a food chain. Each plant and animal is a vital link in the chain. Human beings, too, are part of many different food chains and webs. Just think what you have eaten in the last few days, and prepare to be amazed!

Glossary

algae   very simple plants found in saltwater and freshwater

ammonium   a chemical made from a mixture of nitrogen and other chemicals

bacteria   microscopic, single-celled living things which are found almost everywhere

baleen plates   bone-like plates in a whale's mouth which it uses to filter out food from the water

biodegradable   materials which rot (decompose) away naturally

biomass   the total amount of each individual type of living thing (plant and animal) in a food chain

boreal   boreal forests are those which grow in a band across the far north (polar region) of the world

browsers   animals that eat the leaves of trees or bushes

camouflaged   the way in which an animal or plant is coloured or patterned to imitate and merge in to its surroundings

carbon   a vitally important chemical element which is found in the bodies of all living things

carbon dioxide   gas that living things breathe out during respiration – plants use it in photosynthesis

carnivores   animals that hunt other animals to eat (they only eat meat)

chlorophyll   a green pigment (colouring) found inside plant cells. It absorbs energy from sunlight for use in photosynthesis.

community   the plants and animals that live in a certain habitat

coniferous   trees like pine trees which produce cones

consumers   animals that feed directly on plants, or indirectly by eating other animals

deciduous   trees and plants that regularly shed their leaves

decompose   another word that means to rot or break down

echinoderms   invertebrate animals that live in the sea – for example, starfish, sea-urchins, sea cucumbers

ecosystem   a community of animals and plants and the habitat they live in

entrails   an animal's innards or guts

evergreen   trees and plants that keep their leaves all year round

forage   to collect or search for food

fungi   a kingdom or group of living things which includes mushrooms, toadstools and moulds

glucose   a simple sugar – organisms like plants store food as glucose

grasslands   large, open, flat areas covered in grasses and low bushes. Grasslands cover about a quarter of the land on Earth.

grazers   animals that eat or graze on grass

habitat   a particular area in which certain plants and animals live

herbivores   animals that feed entirely on plants

hibernating   when an animal's body functions slow right down to allow the animal to survive periods of intense cold when food is scarce

humus   rich, dark material made from the rotting bodies of dead plants and animals

invertebrates   animals which do not have backbones or skeletons inside their bodies

kingdom   in scientific classification, the largest group of living things. The five kingdoms include plants, animals and fungi.

larvae   a stage in the life cycle of some animals. Larvae are young forms that look very different from the adults.

nitrates   a form of nitrogen found in the soil

nitrogen   a colourless gas which living things need for growth

nutients   substances in food that a body needs to function

omnivores   animals that feed on both plants and animals

photosynthesis   the process by which green plants make food from carbon dioxide and water, using energy from sunlight absorbed by their chlorophyll

phytoplankton   microscopic, single-celled plants which live in the sea and form the start of the ocean food chain

pigment   a natural colouring or dye

predators   animals which hunt and kill other animals for food

prey   animals that are hunted and eaten by other animals

proboscis   a long, hollow tube, like a tongue, through which butterflies drink nectar and water

producers   all green plants which make their own food by photosynthesis. They start off every food chain.

proteins   chemical substances which living things need for growth

pyramid of biomass   a diagram which shows the total amount in terms of the mass of each living thing in a food chain

pyramid of numbers   a diagram which shows the total numbers of each living thing in a food chain

recycling   the way in which materials are broken down and re-used again and again

saprophytes   living things that feed on dead or decaying plant matter

scavengers   animals that feed on the dead bodies of other animals or plants

shoal   a large number of fish which swim and live together

temperate   places that have cold winters and warm summers. They are found between the hot tropics and the cold Polar regions.

zooplankton   tiny sea animals which graze on the phytoplankton

Index